Is Your Storytale Dragging?

by Jean Stangl

Fearon Teacher Aids
Simon & Schuster Supplementary Education Group

Designer and illustrator: Walt Shelly

ISBN 0-8224-3904-2

Printed in the United States of America

1. 9 8 7 6 5

Contents

Introduction

Are you looking for new ways to perk up your story hour, ways to keep your listeners interested and excited? There are thousands of good children's books on the market today, and books should certainly be an important part of all story programs. But if your program consists only of reading books, and perhaps a flannel graph or puppet story now and then, your students are missing out on a vital link to the world of children's literature—oral storytelling.

Is Your Storytale Dragging? is filled with ideas, suggestions, and stories for oral storytelling that will capture and hold the attention of your young audience. The innovative presentation methods, simple props, and original stories in this book will bring a touch of magic to your story time.

An effective visual aid or prop that accompanies a story not only enhances the story but can also become an important learning tool for helping young children discover art, science, and movement concepts. Visual aids can also develop listening and sequencing skills, improve visual memory, and instill a love for oral storytelling. Students become active participants as they join in repeating phrases, performing the actions of the story, or eating the props!

Remember that props and visual aids should not be overused. A good storyteller leaves plenty of room for the audience's imagination. Telling the stories and then allowing the children to use the props to retell the stories or to create their own tales will be a strong motivator for developing reading and creative writing skills.

These stories are for oral storytelling; they should not be read. Know your story well but don't memorize anything but the repetitious phrases, rhymes, and chants. Read the story a few times and prepare your props ahead of time. You may wish to make a few notes or an outline of the story on 3″ × 5″ cards. As a storyteller, it is your prerogative to alter parts of the story to meet the needs of your audience. Many of the stories in this book can easily be shortened or lengthened.

Illustrations and patterns are provided to help you present the twenty-six stories. At the end of each story, you will also find a follow-up activity which provides children with a related creative experience.

I hope that the stories and props in this book will encourage you and your young audience to tell and create stories. *Is Your Storytale Dragging?* provides you with a valuable guide for introducing children to the exciting art of oral storytelling. Don't let your story time drag!

Part 1

Draw Me a Story

Draw Me a Story

One technique for enlivening a story is to illustrate it as you tell it. You don't have to be able to draw to use this technique. Many stories can be illustrated in advance and then redrawn during the storytelling. With an overhead projector, you can enlarge a drawing, then trace it with chalk on a sheet of newsprint. Place the newsprint on an easel at a distance so the children can see the board but not the chalk drawing. As you tell the story, go over the chalk outline with a felt-tipped pen. Omit the details; illustrate only the basic figure. Simplifying the drawing will make it easier for you during the storytelling and will leave room for the audience's imagination. You can also make dot-to-dot outlines in advance and connect the dots during the storytelling.

Coloring books are one of the best sources for patterns. You can also check magazines, bulletin boards, pattern books, and children's books. Select characters and objects that have few details, pictures that can be drawn one portion at a time as the story evolves. If the main character in the story is a person, consider using stick figures.

The stories in this section provide story illustrations and directions for drawing them. If you wish, you may do a freehand drawing of your own instead.

The following books by Ed Emberley are good sources for drawing books: *Ed Emberley's Little Drawing Book of Animals, Ed Emberley's Little Drawing Book of Farms,* and *Ed Emberley's Little Drawing Book of Trains* (all published by Little, Brown). *The Maid and the Mouse and the Odd-Shaped House,* by Paul Zelinsky (Dodd, Mead), and *Tell and Draw Stories,* by Margaret Olson (Creative Storytime Press), are also fine choices for drawing stories.

Little Bunny

You will need chalk, a chalkboard, and an eraser.
Follow the directions and draw as indicated.

I saw a little bunny,
(Draw head and body.)

Resting by a tree.
(Draw tree.)

I called to the bunny,
(Draw hind feet.)

"Please come and play with me."
(Draw front arms.)

He perked up two long ears,
(Draw ears.)

And shook his fuzzy tail.
(Draw tail.)

He turned to look at me,
(Erase tail. Add eyes, nose, mouth, and whiskers.)

And then ran down the trail.
(Erase bunny.)

Round-Faced Owl

You will need chalk and a chalkboard, or newsprint and a felt-tipped pen. Follow the directions and draw as indicated.

Round-faced owl,
They say you're wise.
(Draw head.)

And that you have
Two great big eyes.
(Draw eyes and beak.)

You sit all night
Up in a tree.
(Draw body with wings.)

And from your limb
You hoot at me.
(Draw limb and feet.)

Activity:

Have children write an owl or bunny rhyme. Suggest to older children that they write a poem and make a drawing about a fish, bird, giraffe, or some other animal.

Spring Is Sprung

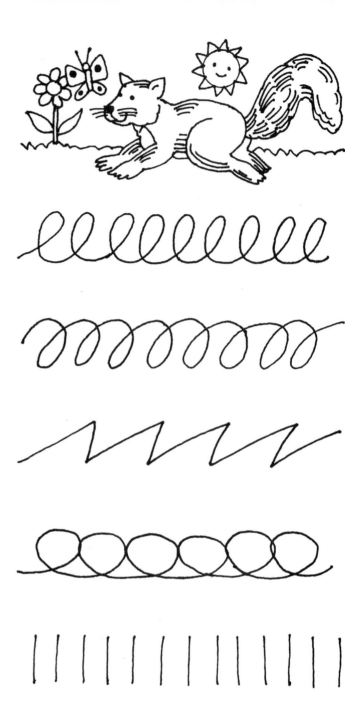

You will need chalk and a large chalkboard, or newsprint on an easel and a felt-tipped pen. Say each line, emphasizing the action word as you do the drawing.

The clouds rolled across the sky.

The thunder rumbled over and over.

The lightning streaked through the heavens.

The wind blew over the land.

The rain fell down.

The sun's rays beamed.

The grass popped up.

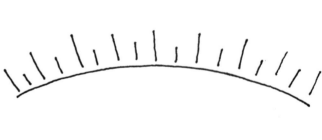

The bunny jumped in the grass.

The butterflies fluttered about.

The bees buzzed in the warm air.

The birds flew from tree to tree.

The spiders spun webs between the flowers.

The squirrel raced around and around.

It's spring! It's spring!

Activity:

Give children large sheets of paper to practice the drawing as you read the story. Have them suggest additional signs of spring and ways to draw them. Older children can create a similar story about one of the other seasons.

Teddy's New House

(an adaptation from an anonymous tale)

You will need one large sheet of newsprint (or other paper) on an easel, chalk, and a felt-tipped pen. Make an enlarged chalk tracing of the cat pattern on page 10 on the newsprint in advance. As you tell the story, draw as indicated.

T is for Teddy, who lives right here.
(Connect d-a, e-1.)

S is for Sara, who lives right here.
(Connect 0-2 with an "S" curve.)

Teddy went to visit Sara.
(Connect 1-2.)

"I have a new house," said Teddy.

"What does it look like?" asked Sara.

"Come with me and I'll show you," Teddy said.

As they walked along, Sara said, "Tell me about your new house."
(Retrace 0-2.)

Teddy said, "Well, it has two rooms,
(Connect 3-4 and 5-6-7-8.)

and two windows,
(Connect 9-10 and 11-12.)

and two chimneys,
(Connect 13-14-15-16 and 17-18.)

and a lot of grass."
(Draw lines for the feet.)

"Let's hurry," said Sara. Teddy and Sara ran down the path. Sara saw Teddy's new house. It had two rooms,
(Connect a–b–c–d.)

and two windows,
(Draw two circles for eyes.)

and two chimneys,
(Draw two triangles for ears.)

and a lot of grass.
(Draw whiskers.)

But before they reached Teddy's new house, they stopped to play with his new . . .
(Connect 1–17, 2–3, and 10–11.)

CAT—meow!

Activity:

Challenge students to draw a figure or design using their initials, a numeral, or a geometric shape as the starting point.

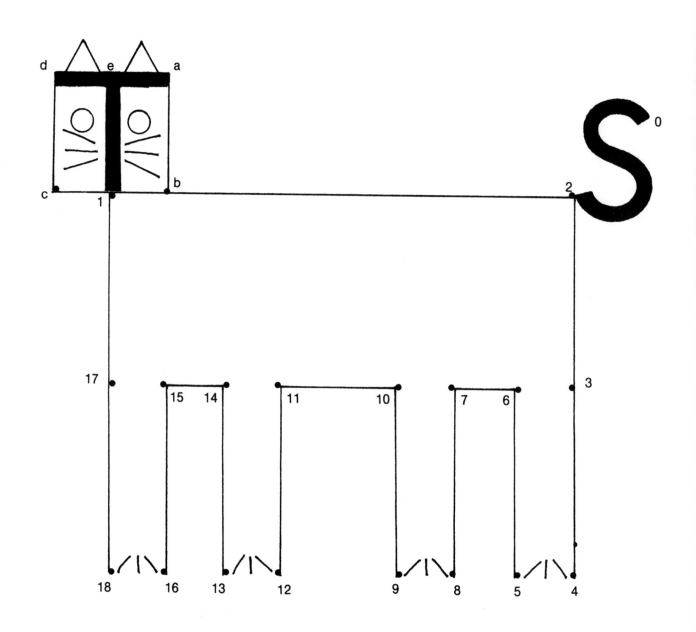

What Am I?

You will need a white crayon, an easel with newsprint, a paintbrush, and diluted yellow paint. Draw the picture with white crayon as you give the clues.

Spider

I have more than four legs.

I am not an insect.

I build traps to catch my food.

I make my own house.

And in the early morning dew,

My house looks like silver lace.

What am I?

(Slowly brush over the drawing with the yellow paint as you repeat the clues.)

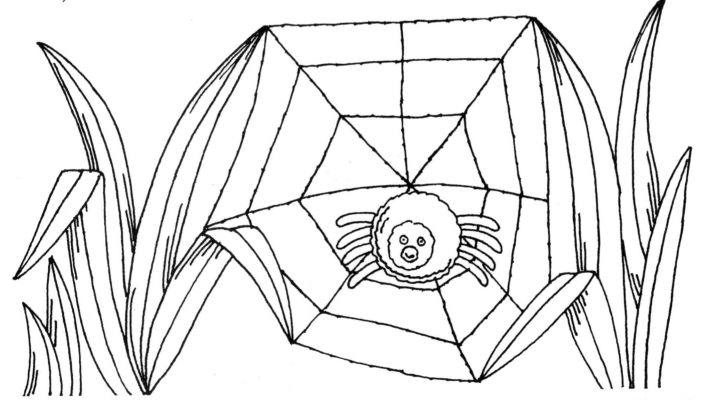

Snail

I have no nose, ears, or legs.

I have over two thousand teeth.

But you can't see them.

I am found all over the world.

I build and carry my own house.

What am I?

(Slowly brush over the drawing with the yellow paint as you repeat the clues.)

Activity:

Have the children create clues for an easy-to-draw animal or object riddle. They can take turns presenting their riddles with or without a drawing.

Part 2

Paper Folding, Tearing, and Cutting Stories

Paper Folding, Tearing, and Cutting Stories

A plain piece of paper that is folded, torn, or cut can be both an attention-getter and a visual aid for reinforcing your story. Select a simple paper prop that you can manipulate easily while telling the story.

Paper folding ideas can be found in origami or other paper folding books such as *Origami*, by Florence Sakade (Charles E. Tuttle Co.), in three volumes; *Origami Made Easy*, by Kunihiko Kasahara (Japan Publications U.S.A.); *Origami: The Art of Paper Folding*, by Robert Harbin (Funk & Wagnalls); and *Paper Folding for Beginners*, by William Murray (Dover).

For paper tearing, use lightweight construction paper, tissue paper, newspaper, wallpaper, or gift wrapping paper. Select a story that contains objects with easy-to-tear outlines. Make your pattern from a picture book illustration or choose one from a coloring or pattern book. Trace the pattern on a piece of paper using chalk or pencil. With a little practice, you will be able to tear your own patterns. Add a loop of tape to the back of the torn illustration and attach it to a piece of poster board.

It Looks Like Spilt Milk, by Charles Shaw (Harper & Row), and *The Very Hungry Caterpillar*, by Eric Carle (World), are good choices for paper-tearing stories.

Almost any kind of paper works for a paper-cutting story. If the paper will be folded several times, use a lightweight paper such as tissue paper. Choose a story with one main character or a surprise figure. Trace your pattern onto a folded sheet of paper and cut portions of the figure as you tell the story. If only straight-line cutting is required, make an outline of dots on the paper and cut dot-to-dot.

Thirty-one paper-cutting stories and rhymes can be found in *Paper Stories* by Jean Stangl (David S. Lake Publishers). *Fold-and-Cut Stories and Fingerplays*, by Marj Hart (David S. Lake Publishers), has seventeen stories and poems with paper-cutting illustrations.

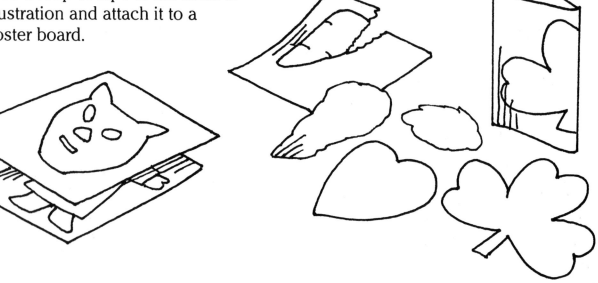

Sailor Boy

(paper folding)

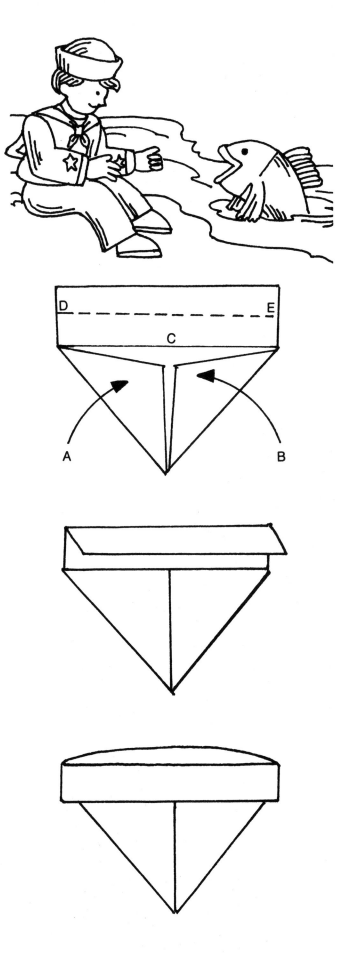

You will need one 8½" x 11" sheet of newsprint. Duplicate the pattern on page 17 on the newsprint. As you tell the story, fold the paper as indicated.

Once there was a tiny boy no bigger than your fist. *(Fold newsprint in half along line A–B. With the folded edge facing you, fold A to C and B to C.)* He lived near a small river that fed into the sea. The tiny boy wanted to be a sailor and sail far away. *(Fold one side of the open edge down along line D–E. Turn the paper over and turn the other edge down.)*

But the people said, "We are too far from the sea and a boat could never come into so small a river. And, tiny boy, you are much too small. You will never be a sailor." *(Fold both folded edges down once again to form a hat.)*

Every morning the tiny boy put on his sailor hat *(place the hat on your head)* and went down to the river. He sat all day on the river bank waiting for a boat to sail in. At night he went home. Day after day he went to the river, but the boat never came.

One day while he was waiting and watching, a giant fish swam up through the water. The fish said, "Tiny boy, if you will pull this hook from my mouth, I will grant you a wish."

The boy pulled out the hook.

"Thank you," said the fish. "What do you wish?"

"I wish that I could be a sailor and sail far out to sea," answered the boy.

"Take off your hat and set it in the water," said the fish.

And the tiny boy did. *(Remove the hat from your head and lay it on its side on the table.)*

The fish swam around and around the hat. Faster and faster it went.

As the boy watched *(turn the hat point down and pull out on the sides to make a boat)*, the hat turned into a boat—a boat just the right size for the tiny boy.

"Jump in," said the fish.

The boy climbed into the boat and sailed away. And off swam the fish. *(Push the boat about on the table.)* Down the river and out into the sea the boy sailed in his very own boat. Up and over the white-capped waves they went. The tiny boy sailed all through the day.

As evening came, a gust of wind turned the boat around and blew it back across the sea and up the river to where the tiny boy lived. *(Push the sides of the boat in and lay it on the table.)*

The boy climbed out of the boat, put on his hat *(place the hat on the top of your head),* and went home.

Activity:

Provide newsprint or sheets of newspaper and show children how to fold the paper into a hat and then into a boat. Children may also wish to decorate their hats and boats.

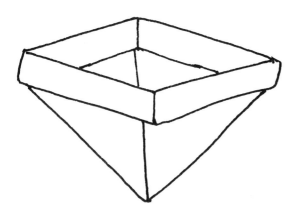

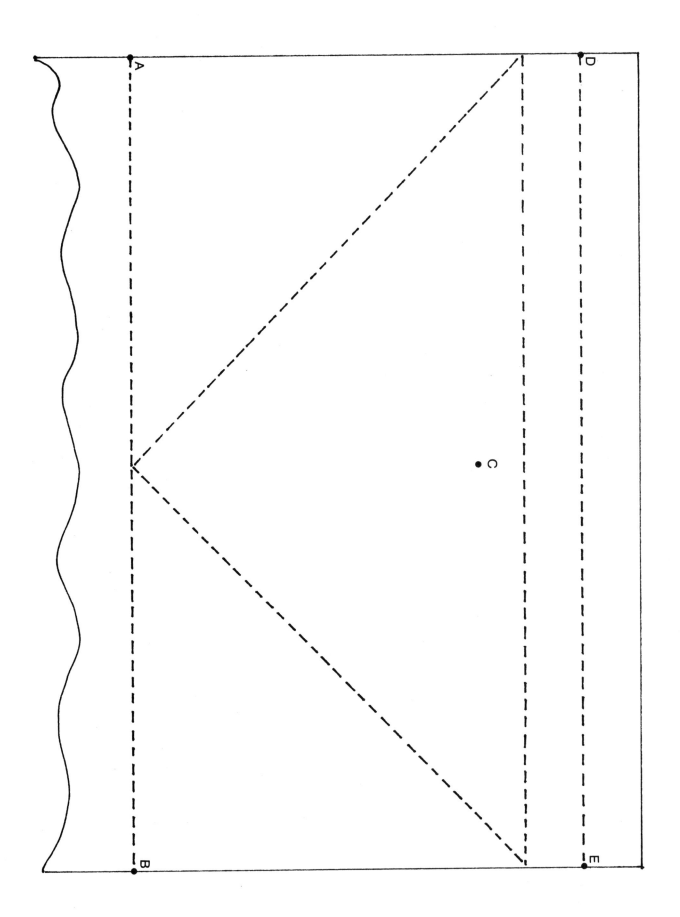

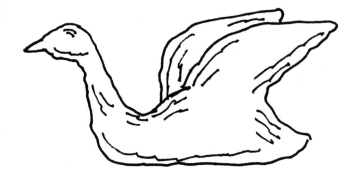

The Silver Night-Shadow

(foil folding)

You will need two 18″ × 24″ sheets of aluminum foil and one half sheet of newspaper. Read the directions in the story for forming the foil into a swan.

Before presenting the story, practice making the swan, using the drawing below for reference.

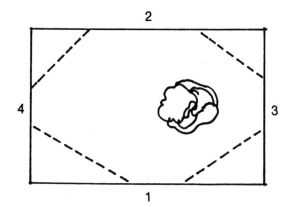

Wings: Pull the two sides *(1 and 2)* up over the foil-covered newspaper and bend them outward to form the wings.

Tail: Form the tail *(3)* by crushing and pinching the foil.

Neck: Crush and bend the front *(4)* into a long arching neck.

Head: Form the end of the neck into a head with a beak.

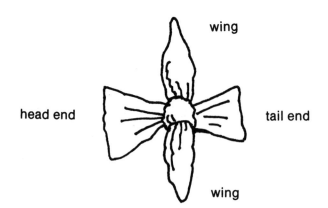

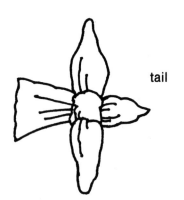

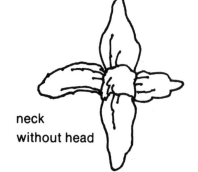

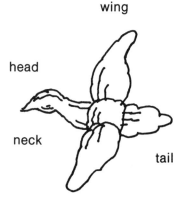

Casey climbed into his boat and rowed out to sea. It was his job to check the fishing nets every night. *(Crush the newspaper tightly, wrap it in foil, and place it as shown on the other foil sheet.)* One night, when the moon was full, he looked far ahead of the boat *(fold out the wings)*, and saw a shadow of silver wings upon the water. The young boy began to row toward the shadow. Harder and harder he pulled on the oars. But before he was able to reach them, the silver wings moved away, farther and farther, until he could no longer see them.

The following night, Casey saw in the distance a shadow that looked like a silver tail. *(Form the tail.)* It sat a little above the water and flipped up and down. *(Move tail up and down.)* The boy began to row with all his strength toward the silver tail, but like the wings, it floated out of sight.

The next night the boy went out again. After checking the nets, he saw a shadow that looked like a long, silver neck. *(Twist and bend the foil to form a long neck and a head.)* The shadow bounced up and down on the water. *(Move head up and down.)* Quickly, Casey rowed toward it. But the faster he rowed, the farther away the silver shadow seemed to move. Finally, it moved out of sight.

And then one night when Casey was checking the nets and the full moon was high in the sky, he saw it clearly. It wasn't a shadow; it was a beautiful, silver night-swan! *(Arch the neck and lift the wings.)* Casey rowed with all his might. Harder and harder he pulled on the oars. Faster and faster he rowed. There it was, right in front of him. Casey reached for it. But the swan floated off. *(Bend the neck and wings in and slowly move the swan behind you.)*

Many times after that night, when the moon was full, Casey saw the beautiful, silver night-swan. *(Return swan to view.)* But every time he rowed near it, it floated off into the night. *(Move swan behind you.)*

Activity:

Provide sheets of aluminum foil and newspaper so the children can create their own silver swans. With a little practice, children will be able to make eagles, chickens, ducks, and other birds.

Mrs. Rabbit's Mixed-Up Garden

(paper tearing)

You will need masking tape; one piece of poster board; and one sheet each of orange, red, white, and beet-red (maroon) 8½″ × 11″ lightweight construction paper. Fold each piece of paper lengthwise and trace the vegetable patterns on page 22.

Mrs. Rabbit heard a rattling sound as she pulled the long, brown package from her mailbox. "The new seeds for my spring garden have finally arrived," she said to herself.

Carefully, Mrs. Rabbit pulled out the tiny seed packages. They were all empty. "Oh, goodness, the packages have broken open and all the seeds have spilled out into the box. How will I know which seeds are which?" she said.

But Mrs. Rabbit decided to plant the mixed-up seeds anyway. She scattered them about in her garden. Then she covered the seeds with soil.

Mrs. Rabbit was a very good gardener. She remembered to water her garden every day and she pulled the weeds, too.

Soon, it was time to harvest the vegetables. Mrs. Rabbit looked at all the green tops in her mixed-up garden and shook her head.

She pulled and pulled on the green tops and up came a *(tear the orange paper according to the pattern to form a carrot)* carrot!

She pulled and pulled on the green tops and up came a *(tear the red paper according to the pattern to form a radish)* radish!

She pulled and pulled on the green tops and up came a *(tear the white paper according to the pattern to form a turnip)* turnip!

She pulled and pulled on the green tops and up came a *(tear the beet-red paper to form a beet)* beet!

And then Mrs. Rabbit fixed herself a fresh vegetable dinner. *(Add a loop of masking tape to each vegetable and tape it to the piece of poster board.)*

Activity:

Have children make their own "tearing garden" by tearing out shapes of their favorite fruits and vegetables and pasting them onto a large sheet of paper. Green tops, trees, and leaves can be added with felt-tipped pens or crayons.

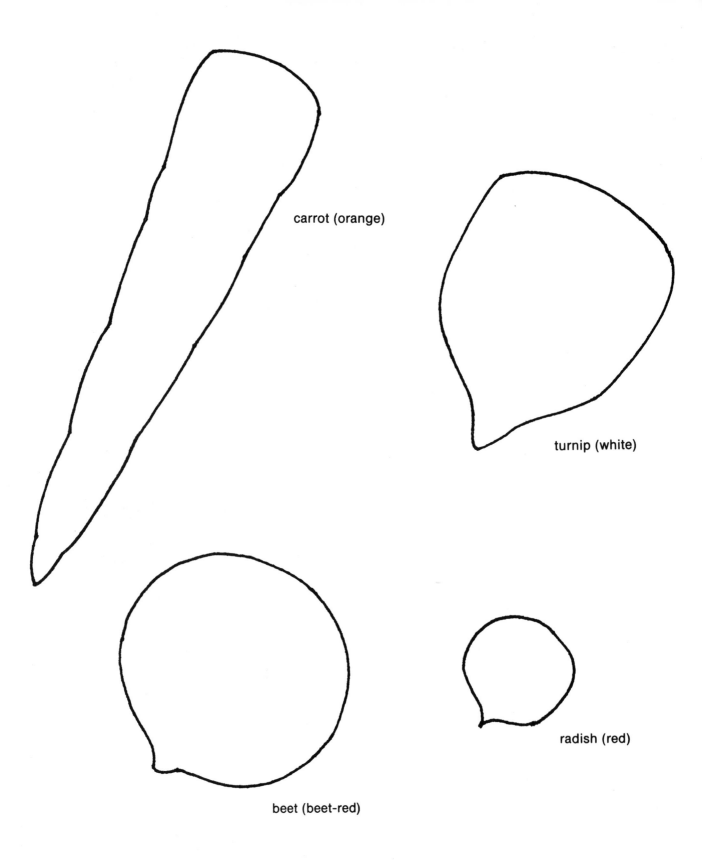

carrot (orange)

turnip (white)

beet (beet-red)

radish (red)

Pam's Magic Trick

(paper tearing)

You will need scissors, black paint, a paintbrush, a large grocery bag, a pencil, and three 8½" x 11" sheets of white tracing paper. Roll down the top of the grocery bag to make a hat brim. Paint the bag black. Fold each piece of paper in half, lengthwise. Trace the rabbit pattern on page 26 on one of the pieces of folded paper. For Pam's first two attempts, tear the paper into any shape, keeping your hands inside the hat. For the third attempt, tear the paper along the rabbit pattern, keeping your hands inside the hat.

"I've decided on my magic trick for the school party," Pam called to her brother. "I am going to pull a rabbit from a hat."

Herbie laughed. "You will never be able to do that," he said.

Pam sat down to study the magic book. She memorized the magic words: "Abracadabra, alakazam, rabbit, rabbit, appear for Pam." Pam borrowed her dad's old hat. *(Set hat on side of table with the hole facing up.)* She got up early each morning to practice. She practiced late into the night.

"Let me see your magic trick," said Herbie.

"No," said Pam. "No one gets to see it until tomorrow at the school party."

The next day, everyone gathered at the party. When it was Pam's turn, she said, "I'll say a few magic words and then I'll pull a rabbit from this black hat." *(Move the hat in front of you.)* She picked up a piece of folded paper and dropped it into the hat. *(Drop first piece of paper into hat.)*

Pam placed her hands into the hat and stirred the paper around and around. *(Place your hands in the hat and tear the paper into an abstract form.)* Then she threw up her hands and repeated the magic words, "Abracadabra, alakazam, rabbit, rabbit, appear for Pam."

Pam reached into the hat and pulled out a—*(pull paper from hat and unfold).*

The class laughed and laughed.

Pam tried it again. She picked up another piece of folded paper and dropped it into the hat. *(Drop in the second sheet of paper.)* Again Pam placed her hands into the hat and stirred the paper around and around. *(Place your hands into the hat and tear the paper into an abstract form.)* She threw up her arms and said, "Abracadabra, alakazam, rabbit, rabbit, appear for Pam."

Pam reached into the hat and pulled out a—*(pull paper from hat and unfold).* The children laughed harder and they booed and hissed. But Pam knew she could do the trick. "Wait," she said, "I know

what's wrong. *You* have to say the magic words."

Pam took a deep breath and tried again. She took another piece of folded paper and dropped it into the hat. *(Drop the piece of paper with the rabbit pattern on it into the hat.)* Pam placed her hands into the hat. *(Place your hands in the hat and tear the paper along the rabbit pattern.)* She stirred the paper around and around and around. She looked up at her classmates and then gave the paper one more good stirring. Everyone was quiet. Pam was sure she had the instructions right, but she kept stirring. Then she threw up her hands and pointed to the children. Together they all called out, "Abracadabra, alakazam, rabbit, rabbit, appear for Pam."

Pam reached into the hat. She felt all around and then she pulled out—*(pull paper from the hat, unfold it, and show the three rabbits)*—three rabbits.

The children cheered and clapped their hands. Pam was a real magician!

Activity:

Have each child make a magic hat, write a story, and create an appropriate paper-tearing figure. Have a class magic party.

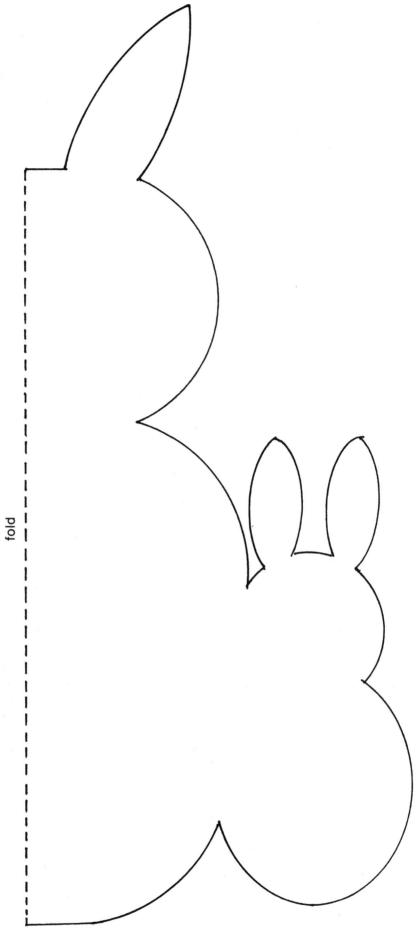

fold

Barney's Mission

(paper cutting)

You will need an 8½" x 11" sheet of green construction paper and a pair of scissors. Duplicate the shamrock pattern on page 29 on the green construction paper so that the dotted line runs down the center. Cut as indicated in the story.

Many years ago, in a deep forest of Ireland, there lived a special family of leprechauns called the Deep Forest Leprechauns. No one had ever seen them, for they only traveled at night. All the people of Ireland hoped that one day they would be lucky enough to be visited by one of the Deep Forest Leprechauns. *(Fold paper on the dotted line.)*

It was mid-March when a wise old leprechaun called one of the youngest leprechauns, Barney, to his side.

"Barney," he said, "you have been chosen for an important mission. Tonight you will deliver this box to Paddy Flannigan, who lives on the far side of the valley. You must not take a light. Make sure that no one sees you."

Barney's face lit up. He had waited a long time for his first mission. "Thank you," he said. "I'll be ready to go as soon as it's dark."

That night, Barney took the box and set out on his mission. He climbed up the mountain and slid down the other side. *(Cut 1-2.)*

He jumped over the bubbling brook. *(Cut 2-3.)* In and around the tall trees he went. *(Cut 3-4.)* Once he tripped and nearly dropped the little box. *(Cut 4-5.)*

Barney was tired, so he sat down on a rock to rest. *(Cut 5-6.)* But he knew his family was depending on him, so he had to go on. Down through the potato fields he walked, and then across a small bridge. *(Cut out section 7.)*

At last he came to the narrow lane that led to a small white cottage. It was almost midnight when he reached Paddy Flannigan's house. Barney climbed in the open window. Paddy Flannigan was sleeping soundly. Barney placed the box on the table near the bed. Then he tiptoed to the window and jumped out. *(Cut out section 8.)* Now that his mission was finished, Barney could return home.

The next morning, Paddy Flannigan awoke to the sun streaming through the open window. *(Cut out section 9.)* And he was happy, too, for he saw the tiny box on the table. Paddy Flannigan knew that he had been visited by one of the Deep Forest Leprechauns. The happy man opened up the box and found inside his very own *(unfold the paper)* good luck shamrock.

Activity:

Challenge children to write their own "cutting story" about one of the symbols of Ireland—pipe, snake, potato, or hat.

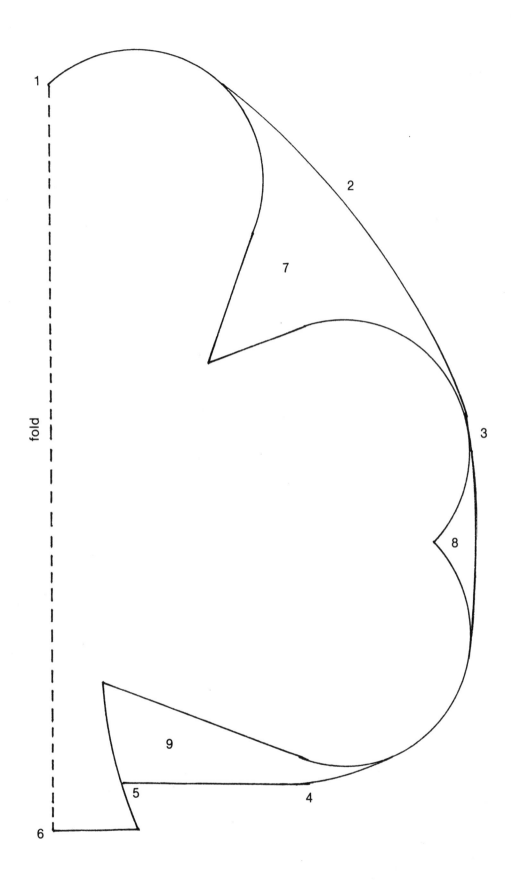

fold

The Green-Eyed Monster

(paper cutting)

You will need scissors, white chalk, a green crayon, and one 8½″ x 11″ sheet of black construction paper. Fold your paper from top to bottom. Cut out the pattern on page 32 and mark the dots on the folded paper with white chalk. Turn the paper over and outline the *Y* space. As you tell the story, cut as directed.

Kenny and Joseph decided to sleep outside. They set up their tent in the middle of the backyard. *(Cut out the* X *section.)*

"I'll unroll my sleeping bag here," said Kenny.

"And here's a good place for mine," Joseph said.

Kenny and Joseph crawled into their sleeping bags and turned off the flashlight.

"What's that noise?" whispered Joseph.

Kenny turned on the flashlight and shone it around the yard *(Cut 1-2.)* The light shook in his hand.

High up in a tree *(cut 2-3),* they saw two green, shiny eyes staring down at them.

"It's a monster," said Kenny, his voice shaking.

"A monster with green eyes," Joseph said.

The green-eyed monster took one giant leap from the tree and landed on the fence rail. *(Cut 3-4.)* It moved along the fence. *(Cut 4-5.)* The boys

followed it with the beam of the flashlight.

The pair of eyes turned the corner (cut 5-6) and moved silently down the long side of the fence. (Cut 6-7.)

Crash! The monster knocked a can of paint off the fence and it fell, SPLASH, right here and right here. (Color both Y spaces green and show the green spots to the children. Don't unfold the paper.)

"Where did it go?" ased Kenny. "I can't see it."

"There it is, in the bushes," answered Joseph. (Cut 7-8.)

"Watch out!" yelled Kenny. "It's coming this way." (Cut 8-9.)

The two boys huddled close together inside their tent. Their teeth were chattering and their hearts were pounding.

The green eyes moved closer (cut 9-10) and closer (cut 10-11). They came right into the tent! (Cut 11-12.)

"Ooooooooooooo," said the boys.

The green-eyed monster was only a . . . (unfold the paper) cat.

Activity:

Provide children with scissors, a copy of the pattern, a green crayon, and a black crayon. Retell the story, pausing to give cutting directions. Color the cat black, and add green eyes.

The cutout can also be made into a cat mask. Cut out the Y spaces and outline each eye with a green crayon. Punch holes on each side of the mask, attach rubber bands, and tie the two bands together to fit the child's head.

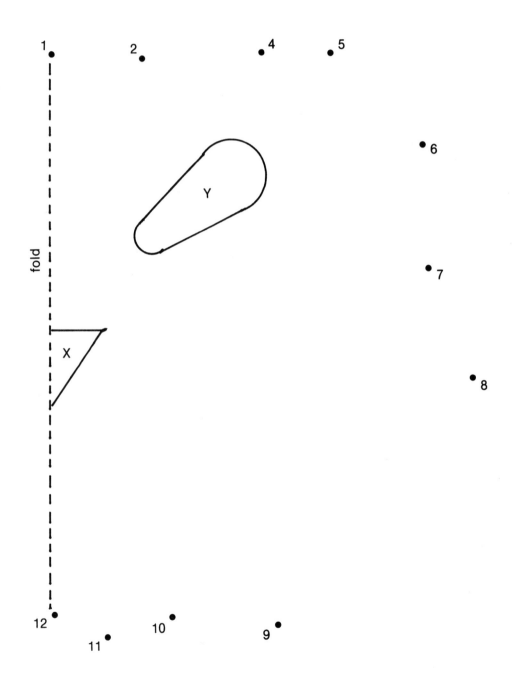

fold

3
1   2   4   5

6

Y

7

8

X

12
11   10   9

Is Your Storytale Dragging? © 1988

Nibble, Nibble

(paper cutting)

You will need scissors and a 6″ square of white tracing paper. Duplicate the pattern on page 34 on the tracing paper. Fold along fold lines #1, #2, and #3. Hold the paper at the pointed corner as you tell the story and cut according to the directions.

Softly and gently it fell, down, down, into the hole where Tiny Mouse lived. He could not see what it was, for his underground house was very dark.

Tiny Mouse sniffed the strange object. It had no smell but it felt very cold against his nose. "What is it?" he wondered. Tiny Mouse took a bite. *(Cut 1-2.)*

The little mouse was puzzled. He opened his mouth wide and took a giant-sized bite like this. *(Cut 3-4-5.)*

Using his sharp front teeth, he sliced off one edge and then the other. *(Cut 1-6 and 7-8.)*

Quickly, Tiny Mouse began to nibble down the other side. Nibble, nibble, nibble. *(Cut out the 9s.)* Next, he bit off the corner. *(Cut on line 10.)*

Tiny Mouse was getting tired. He chewed on the other side. Chomp, chomp. *(Cut out the 11s.)*

Tiny Mouse decided to take two final nibbles—a little nibble here *(cut out 12)* and a little nibble here *(cut out 13)*. Then it was gone. It seemed to have melted away!

What was Tiny Mouse nibbling on? *(Slowly unfold paper.)* A snowflake.

Activity:

Provide children with tracing or tissue paper and scissors. Demonstrate the folding technique and then let the children cut snowflakes in their choice of size and design.

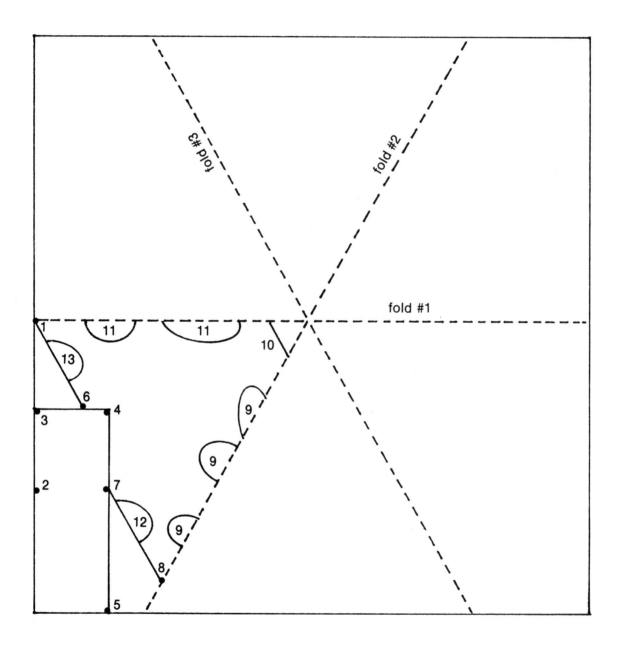

Part 3

Flip Chart Stories

Flip Chart Stories

Used as a storytelling prop, a flip chart consists of several sheets of paper containing a sequence of pictures. The pages are fastened together at the top with two large rings. As the story unfolds, the storyteller flips each page.

The flip chart can be any size. Sheets of white paper, colored construction paper, and tagboard work equally well. Six to eight pages are usually sufficient. Unless the story requires one, a cover is not needed. However, if you make a front and a back cover out of heavy cardboard, you can use them as a stand. The chart can also be held in your lap or set on an easel.

Select large, colorful pictures from magazines, newspapers, seed catalogs, or old picture books. You need only the main characters or objects. Patterns can

be found in coloring books or pattern books. Color or paint the pictures, or draw your own. Remember that you are not illustrating a book but providing a prop that will hold the attention of your listeners and stimulate their imaginations.

After completing the pictures, assemble them in the correct sequence, punch two holes at the top, and insert a ring through each hole. Make sure the rings are large enough for the pages to be flipped through easily.

Imagination

A Color Story

You will need two large rings, a hole punch, and one sheet of paper in each of the following colors: white, red, green, gray, pink, blue, purple, yellow, gold, orange, brown, and silver. Select bright, clear colors. For gold and silver, spray paint a sheet of white paper. Arrange the colors as listed. For the top cover, use either a multicolored sheet or make a collage of the twelve colors. Punch two holes at the top and insert a large ring through each.

Ask the children, "What is imagination?" After some discussion, tell the children that they will need to use their imaginations for this story. Turn to the white page and start the story. Flip the page as you mention each new month. Pause to allow the children to name each color.

In January we see . . . white.

In our imaginations, we see fluffy white snowflakes falling gently, gently to the ground. Drifts of snow piled against the fence. Children running and playing in the fresh snow. Snowballs and snowpeople. Clean, cold snow to eat.

In February we see . . . red.

In our imaginations, we see red valentines: large red ones and small red ones. Cupids and arrows and love, love, love. A big red valentine box filled with lacy red valentines.

In March we see . . . green.

In our imaginations, we see green trees and green grass. Green shamrocks nodding in the breeze. Little green leprechauns jumping about.

In April we see . . . gray.

In our imaginations, we see gray skies and clouds. Gray, falling rain. Gray umbrellas and gray raincoats. Puddles on the gray sidewalks. Gray water running down the street.

In May we see . . . pink.

In our imaginations, we see pink, budding trees. Tiny pink flowers and large pink roses. A birthday cake with pink candles. Presents with pink ribbons and bows.

In June we see . . . blue.

In our imaginations, we see the clear, blue sky. Blue water of lakes and ponds. And the blue of the calm sea. The bright blue of the flag waving proudly in the breeze.

In July we see . . . purple.

In our imaginations, we see bright purple wildflowers in the field. A purple kite rising in the summer air. Purple sunglasses and purple swimsuits.

In October we see . . . orange.

In our imaginations, we see giant orange pumpkins growing in the fields. Orange pumpkins piled high in the supermarket. Little orange pumpkins carried by children wearing costumes. Candles glowing through the smiling face of an orange jack-o'-lantern.

In August we see . . . yellow.

In our imaginations, we see the bright yellow of the shining sun, its yellow rays warming our faces and arms. The warm, warm sand heated by the yellow sun. A yellow balloon floating off into the sunlight.

In November we see . . . brown.

In our imaginations, we see brown frostbitten grass and plants. The drumstick of the turkey, roasted brown. The delicious smell of brown pumpkin pies and golden-brown sweet potatoes. Hot brown apple cider steaming in a cup.

In September we see . . . gold.

In our imaginations, we see gold leaves hanging on the trees and gold leaves falling to the ground. Goldenrod blooming along the road. Delicious, golden ears of corn dripping with butter the color of gold.

In December we see . . . silver.

In our imaginations, we see a silver garland wrapped around and around the tree. Glittering, silver icicles draped over the branches. Silver bells that ring softly, and shiny silver stars. And on the very top, an angel with widespread, silver wings.

Activity:

Have children choose several pieces of colored paper to construct their own pocket-sized "imagination book." For a creative writing assignment, each student can write a story about his or her favorite color.

Kenna's Yellow Flower

You will need scissors, glue, a felt-tipped pen, two large rings, and white construction paper. Make a nine-page flip chart, 8½″ × 11″. Trace the patterns on page 42 on the construction paper, cut them out, and glue them to the pages as shown. If you prefer, paint or color the patterns, cut pictures from magazines or seed catalogs, or draw your own illustrations. Assemble the pages, punch two holes through the top, and insert a large ring through each hole.

(Page 1.)

"What's that green thing peeking over the fence?" asked Kenna.

"Well now, I'm not sure," answered Mother.

Kenna stood on her tiptoes. "I think it's a leaf, a heart-shaped leaf. Do you think it's a big tree?"

"No, I don't think it's a tree," said Mother.

(Turn to page 2.)

Kenna watched the plant grow. Soon, more leaves appeared above the fence.

(Turn to page 3.)

Kenna's plant grew taller and taller.

(Turn to page 4.)

One morning, Kenna called, "Mommy, come and see the pretty yellow flower on my plant."

(Turn to page 5.)
Every day Kenna went to look at her flower. The plant grew taller and taller. The flower grew bigger and bigger.

In the mornings, when Kenna looked at her pretty yellow flower, it looked right back at her.

(Turn to page 6.)
But in the afternoons, when Kenna looked at her flower, it turned away and she couldn't see it.

"Why does it do that?" Kenna asked.

"Your flower follows the sun," said Mother.

"I know," said Kenna, "it's a sunflower! My flower's a sunflower!"

Mother laughed, "Yes, it *is* a sunflower."

(Turn to page 7.)
The flower grew bigger and bigger.

(Turn to page 8.)
Soon the petals fell off and the flower turned brown. It didn't turn to the sun anymore. The brown flower bent far over the fence and looked down at Kenna.

(Turn to page 9.)
Kenna heard a cracking sound. She looked up. Her flower fell off and dropped at her feet. Kenna picked it up and laughed.

"Mommy, come and see my funny flower," she called.

"Your flower has turned to seeds," Mother said. "When the seeds are dry, you can eat them. Birds like them, too."

"There are hundreds of seeds," said Kenna. "We can eat some and the birds can eat some, but I'll save one to plant so that I can grow another yellow sunflower."

Activity:

Give children sunflower seeds to plant outside in the full sun. Children can illustrate the seed cycle or the plant's growth. Older children can make a bar or picture graph to show how rapidly the sunflower plant grows.

Sprouting seeds in the classroom on a piece of moist cotton is an interesting project for young children. When the sprouts are an inch high, plant the seedlings, with the cotton attached, outside.

Page 1

Page 2

Page 3

Page 4

Page 5

Page 6

Page 7

Page 8

Page 9

Felt-tipped pens can be used to draw stems and the sun.

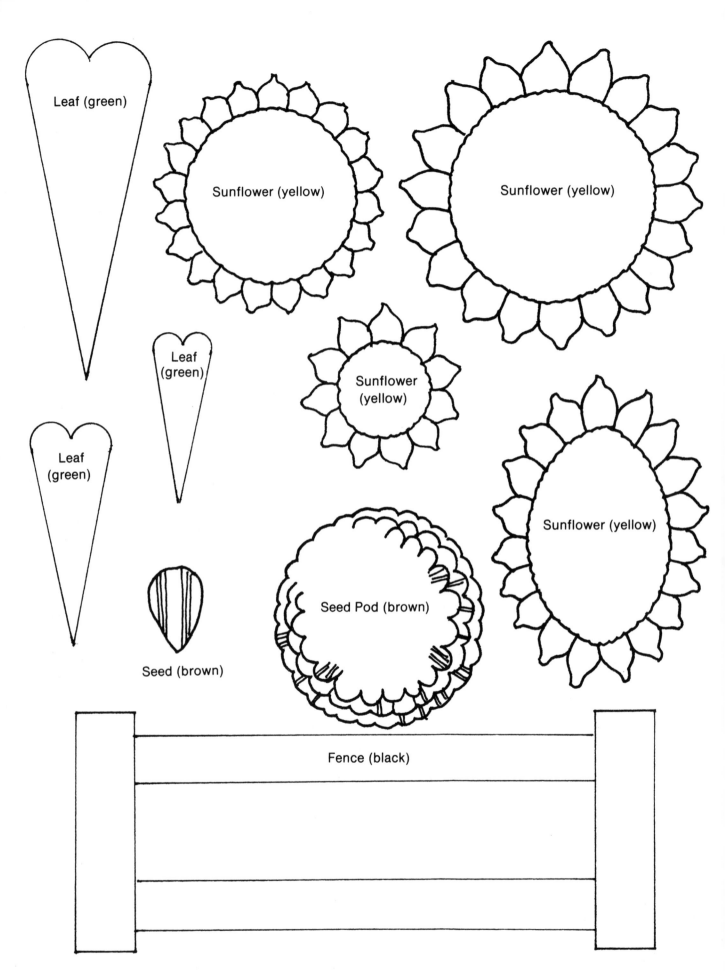

Leaf (green)

Sunflower (yellow)

Sunflower (yellow)

Leaf
(green)

Sunflower
(yellow)

Leaf
(green)

Sunflower (yellow)

Seed (brown)

Seed Pod (brown)

Fence (black)

42   Kenna's Yellow Flower   *Is Your Storytale Dragging?* © 1988

Part 4

String Board Stories

String Board Stories

A string board for storytelling consists of a flat backboard with pockets at the bottom to conceal the main figures of the story. Strings are attached to the main figures and draped over the back of the board. To bring illustrated action to the story, the storyteller pulls the strings up and down, stopping at different levels.

Materials

To construct a five-pocket string board and story figures, you will need the following items: scissors; stapler; glue; a sharp knife; tape; one piece of 4″ × 15″ tagboard for the figures; one 25″ × 20″ piece of heavy poster board; one 30″ × 5″ piece of wallpaper or colored butcher paper; five 30″ pieces of heavy white thread or fishing line; one 40″ piece of colored one-inch plastic tape.

Board

Place the wallpaper across the 25″ bottom of the poster board. Staple it loosely across the bottom and along the two sides. Divide the paper into five pockets by stapling between the pocket sections. The opening of the pockets must allow space for the figures to slide in and out. Cover the three stapled edges with colored plastic tape.

Make five small slits across the top of the board, centering each one over a pocket. Depending on your stories, you may wish to make a board with only three or four pockets.

Figures

Story figures can be drawn freehand; made from patterns found in coloring or pattern books; or cut from discarded picture books, magazines, or catalogs. Cut out five 3″ × 4″ rectangles from tagboard. Round the edges of each piece to form an oval. Trim the story figures and glue them to the tagboard. Tape one end of a thread lengthwise to the center (back side) of each oval (see illustration). The oval shape of the tagboard, with the thread correctly taped, helps to balance the figure and allows it to be pulled smoothly.

Place each figure in a pocket according to its appearance in the story, using a left to right order. Make a hand loop on the other end of each thread. Pull one figure up to the center of the board. Place the thread in the slit. Knot the thread so the knot will catch behind the slit, holding the figure in place. Remove the thread from the slit and pull the figure near the top of the board. Make another knot to hold the figure at this level. Release the thread from the slit before raising or lowering the figure. Prepare each story figure in the same way.

Place the board on an easel, extending several inches above the easel's top. Stand behind the board to operate the strings and tell the story.

One board can be used for all your string board stories. Make a set of figures, with threads attached, for each story. Store each set of figures in a separate envelope.

25"

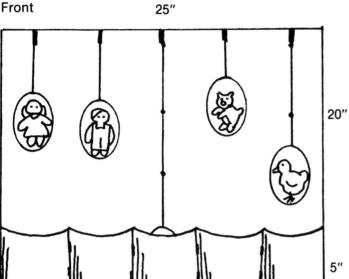

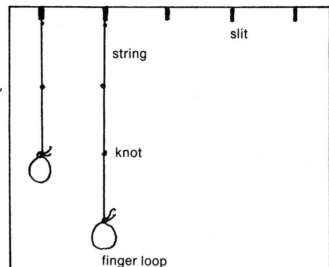

20"

slit

string

knot

5"

finger loop

BOARD

Staple the 30" × 5" piece of wallpaper across the bottom of the poster board. Divide the paper into five pockets by stapling between the pocket sections. Make sure that the top of the pockets will allow the figures to slide in and out easily. Cover the three stapled edges with plastic tape.

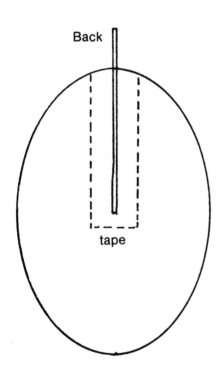

Back

tape

FIGURES

From the tagboard, cut an oval for each figure. Glue story figures to the ovals. Tape the thread lengthwise to the back of each oval as shown. Be sure to center the thread.

Friends in the Park

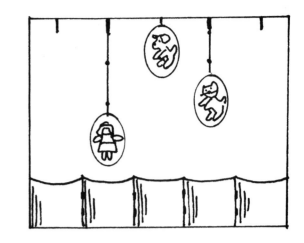

You will need the following string board figures: a girl, a dog, and a cat. Read the instructions for making and using a string board on page 44. Duplicate and cut out the figures on page 48. Glue the figures to oval pieces of tagboard, and tape a thread to the back side of each one. Place, in sequence, the girl, the dog, and the cat in their respective pockets. On the string board, level 1 is in the pocket, level 2 is near the center, and level 3 is near the top. Follow the directions for pulling the string.

One sunny day, a girl went to the park to play. *(Slowly pull girl to level 3.)* But there were no children to play with, so the girl sat on a bench and took a package of cookies from her pocket. *(Lower girl to level 2.)*

Then a dog came to the park to play. *(Slowly pull dog to level 3.)* But there were no dogs in the park to play with, so the dog lay down on the cool grass. *(Lower dog to level 2.)*

The girl watched the dog and munched on her cookie. *(Wiggle girl's string.)* Next, a cat came to the park to play. *(Slowly pull cat to level 3.)* But there were no cats to play with, so the cat stretched out in the warm sun. *(Lower cat to level 2.)*

The girl watched the cat and munched on her cookie. *(Wiggle girl's string.)* Then the girl stood up. *(Pull girl to level 3.)*

"Hey, dog," she called as she held out a cookie.

The dog came and ate the cookie. *(Move dog to level 3.)* The dog licked the girl's hand and the girl patted the dog's head.

"Hey, cat," the girl called as she held out another cookie.

The cat came and ate the cookie. *(Move cat to level 3.)* The cat rubbed against the girl's leg. The girl stroked the cat's back.

Then the girl ran through the park. *(Move girl up and down, stopping at level 2.)* The dog ran after the girl. *(Move dog up and down, stopping at level 2.)* The cat ran after the dog. *(Move cat up and down, stopping at level 2.)*

When they came to the fence, the cat ran back. *(Move cat to level 3.)* The dog ran after the cat. *(Move dog to level 3.)* And the girl ran after the dog. *(Move girl to level 3.)*

The girl, the dog, and the cat played until they were tired. Then the girl went home. *(Move girl to level 1.)* The dog went home. *(Move dog to level 1.)* And the cat went home. *(Move cat to level 1.)*

Activity:

Have children draw or paint a picture about the story. Children can create their own stories about the three characters and then tell their stories using the string board.

Girl

Dog

Cat

Joe and the Snowboy

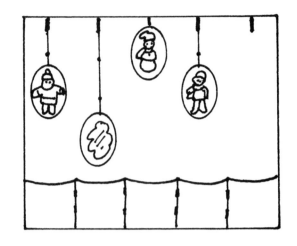

You will need the following string board figures: Joe, the puddle, the snowboy, and the new boy. Read the instructions for making and using a string board on page 44. Duplicate and cut out the figures on page 52. Glue the figures to oval pieces of tagboard, and tape a thread to the back side of each one. Place, in sequence, Joe, the puddle, the snowboy, and the new boy in their respective pockets. On the string board, level 1 is below the middle of the board, level 2 is in the middle of the board, and level 3 is near the top of the board. Follow the directions for pulling the string.

Far up north, in a land of ice and snow, lived a boy named Joe. *(Raise Joe to level 2.)* Joe and his mother and father lived with a few other people in a small village.

One day, because there were no other children to play with, Joe decided to build a snowboy. He packed and rolled the wet snow until he had three balls just the right size. Joe stacked one ball on top of the other and then patted and smoothed the snow. *(Raise the snowboy to level 2.)*

Joe placed his old sock hat on the snowboy. He took the buttons from his dad's old shirt and placed them on the snowboy. His mother gave him an old scarf, which he wrapped around the snowboy's neck. He used an apple peel for a mouth and a pine cone for a nose. It was a fine-looking snowboy.

Every day, Joe talked to his snowboy. Of course, the snowboy never answered, but Joe didn't care. He skated in and around the snowboy *(move Joe slightly up and down)*, and he rode his sled down the hill near the snowboy. *(Raise Joe to level 3 and then lower him to level 1.)* Joe and the snowboy were the very best of friends.

One day late in winter, when the sun was shining over the village, a new boy moved into the empty house across the road. *(Raise the new boy to level 2.)*

"Come over and see my snowboy," Joe called. The boy came over. He and Joe took turns skating and riding the sled. They laughed and played all day. *(Move Joe and the new boy slightly up and down.)*

When it was time to go indoors, the new boy said, "Tomorrow, come over to my house and play."

"Thanks," said Joe, as he waved goodbye. *(Lower boys to pockets.)*

While the boys slept, a warm spring wind blew across the village and melted the snowboy. *(Lower snowboy to pocket.)* The next day, Joe went outside. *(Raise Joe to level 2.)*

His new friend came out and called him over. *(Raise new boy to level 3.)* Joe ran across the road *(raise puddle to level 2),* right past the big puddle of water. *(Raise Joe to level 3.)* He didn't even notice that the snowboy was gone, for now Joe had a real friend to play with.

Activity:

For discussion, ask the children what makes a good friend. Then have them write a letter to a friend.

Joe

Snowboy

Puddle

New Boy

Part 5

Stories You Can Eat

Stories You Can Eat

Stories about food nearly always guarantee a captive audience. When food is used as a prop in a story, your eager listeners will look forward to the snack that is sure to follow.

Using props for "food stories" can be as simple as buying a bakery-made gingerbread boy, or as involved as organizing a classroom project to measure, mix, bake, and decorate gingerbread people.

I have found the following picture books, stories, and props very effective for storytelling sessions:

Bread and Jam for Frances, by Russell and Lillian Hoban (Harper & Row). You will need a jar of jam, a table knife, and several slices of bread. Spread jam on a slice of bread each time "bread and jam" is mentioned in the story. At the end of the story, cut the bread into quarters and serve it to the audience.

The Carrot Seed, by Ruth Krauss (Harper & Row). You will need a package of carrot seeds, a pot of soil, a carrot with the green top attached, and a one-inch piece cut from the top of a carrot that you started growing in a dish of water two weeks in advance. Keep the props out of sight until each is mentioned in the story.

Johnny Appleseed, an American folktale. You will need a cooking pot that fits your head, apple seeds in a plastic bag, and an assortment of apples in a clear plastic bag. Wear your "cooking pot hat" and carry the bag of apples over your shoulder. Each time you mention Johnny planting seeds, pass out a few seeds. Repeat this until everyone has some seeds. When it is time to eat the apples, save the seeds and use them to make a Johnny Appleseed mural for the classroom.

Any picture book or folktale that has a food theme presents a possibility for using food as a prop during the telling of the story.

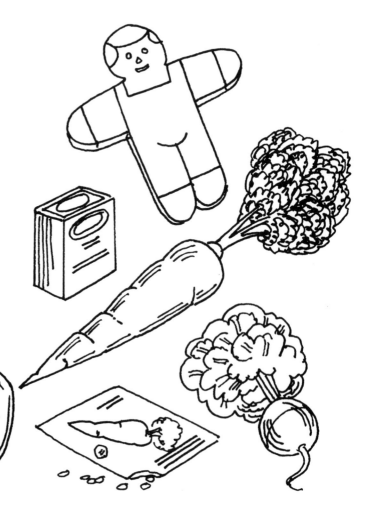

The Giant Fruit Salad

You will need a clear glass punch bowl and ladle, two wooden mixing spoons, plastic serrated picnic knives, paper towels, several small bowls, a plastic spoon and cup for each child, eight or more paper bags, and fresh fruit—apples, oranges, bananas, seedless grapes, pears, and cantaloupe. Other fruit may also be used. The amount needed will depend on the size of the group. Before class, place each kind of fruit in a separate paper bag and tightly twist the top of each bag. Number the bags. Set the bag of apples (number 1) aside. Divide the class into small groups to correspond with the number of bags of fruit. Pass out one bag to each group. Tell the groups to keep their fruit a secret as they work on clues to describe the fruit. Have the students write their clues on paper, and allow sufficient time for group work before you start the story.

Once there was a teacher who went to the store and bought some fruit. Each kind of fruit had been hoping that someone would buy it and that it would become part of a giant fruit salad. But each kind of fruit was in a paper bag, and it could only get out if someone could guess the fruit's name from certain clues.

The teacher took the bags of fruit to school to see if the children could help. The fruit in bag number 1 says *(hold up the bag of apples):*

I'm larger than a golf ball, but smaller than a basketball.

Yet I'm not quite round.

I can be many colors, but never black or white.

My inside is a different color than my outside.

My outside is also good to eat.

(Write the clues on the chalkboard. Ask each group to consider the clues and to write a guess on paper. Then have the groups take turns reading their guesses. Do not give any response to the answers. After the last guess, remove the apples from the bag and place them in the punch bowl.)

The fruit in bag number 2 says: *(Have group 2 read aloud and then write their clues on the chalkboard. Allow time for the other groups to make their decisions, and then have them read their answers. After the last guess, group 2 removes the fruit from the bag and places it in the bowl.)*

The fruit in bag number 3 says: *(Repeat the above instructions until all the groups have had their turn.)*

The fruits were happy that the children had guessed what they were so that they could be released from the paper bags. Now they waited in the bowl, still hoping that one day they would all be made into a giant fruit salad.

Activity:

Provide each group with their original fruit, serrated plastic knives, some paper towels, and a small bowl. Instruct them to wash both their hands and the fruit and then to prepare their fruit for the salad. Empty the small bowls of fruit into the punch bowl. Mix well with the wooden spoons, and have the children use the ladle to serve themselves a cup of their giant fruit salad.

Snow Soup

You will need an old cooking pot and a stick for stirring. Duplicate the patterns on page 60 for tree bark, blueberries, acorns, carrots, and sunflower seeds on colored construction paper. Laminate these items. As you tell the story, stir the soup and add the ingredients as they are mentioned.

One cold winter day, Mr. Fox was plodding through the deep snow near the edge of the forest. Mr. Fox rubbed his empty stomach. "I'm so hungry! I wish I had taken time to store up some food before it started snowing," he said to himself.

Mr. Fox leaned against a pine tree and watched the other animals hurrying down to the stream for fresh water. First came Mrs. Rabbit. "No doubt she has plenty of carrots stored up for the winter," he thought. Down from the tree came Gray Squirrel. "His house must be stuffed with acorns," thought Mr. Fox. Then along came Old Beaver, Mother Bear, and Blue Jay.

"I'm sure they all have extra food stored away," muttered Mr. Fox to himself. "I've got to find some food."

Hungry Mr. Fox reached up and grabbed a handful of green pine needles and stuffed them into his mouth. He quickly spit out the bitter needles. Hoping to find some food, he started digging in the snow. But all he found was an old cooking pot and a few empty cans. *(Place cooking pot on the table.)* He stared at the empty pot and chuckled softly.

Then he began to break off the dead branches from some nearby trees. He stacked the branches into a large pile. Then he filled the old pot with fresh, clean snow and set it on top of the branches. Next, he lit the branches on fire. He picked up a long stick and slowly began to *stir* the snow. The other animals saw the fire and gathered around to watch.

"What are you making?" asked Mother Bear.

"Snow soup," replied Mr. Fox as he continued to stir.

"Now that would be something worth knowing about," said Gray Squirrel.

"If you want to learn how to make it," said Mr. Fox, "just watch me."

Feeling very generous, he invited all the animals to stay for dinner. As he continued to *stir*, he sang:

> Stirring and stirring and stirring the pot,
> I think this soup is getting hot.

"Snow makes good soup, but if we had a few carrots, it would taste much better," said Mr. Fox.

"I have some carrots," said Mrs. Rabbit. She rushed off to get them and soon returned with a nice bunch.

"Why, thank you," said Mr. Fox. He *added the carrots to the soup*. As he continued to *stir*, he sang:

> Stirring and stirring and stirring the pot,
> I think this soup is getting hot.

"Good soup should have a few pieces of tender tree bark for flavor," said Mr. Fox.

Old Beaver was sure he could find some, so off he went. In no time at all, he returned with several pieces of soft tree bark. Mr. Fox *added the bark to the soup*.

"Thank you," said Mr. Fox. As he continued to *stir*, he sang:

> Stirring and stirring and stirring the pot,
> I think this soup is getting hot.

Mr. Fox then looked up and said, "I think this soup could use a few dried berries."

Mother Bear quickly shuffled off to check for some in her cave. Soon she returned with some dried blueberries.

"Thank you," said Mr. Fox, and he *emptied the blueberries into the soup*. As he continued to *stir*, he sang:

> Stirring and stirring and stirring the pot,
> I think this soup is getting hot.

"It's coming along fine," he said. "I think it's almost ready, but a few acorns would improve the flavor."

Gray Squirrel scampered up to his house in the old oak tree and brought back a few crunchy acorns. Mr. Fox *added the acorns to the soup*.

"Thank you," he said. As he continued to *stir*, he sang:

> Stirring and stirring and stirring the pot,
> I think this soup is getting hot.

"If only we had a few sunflower seeds," said Mr. Fox, "I think this soup would be ready to eat."

Swiftly Blue Jay flew off to his nest in a nearby tree. Soon he returned, carrying the sunflower seeds in his beak. Mr. Fox *added the sunflower seeds to the soup.*

"Thank you," he said. As he continued to *stir,* he sang:

Stirring and stirring and stirring the pot,
I think this soup is getting hot.

Then he stopped stirring. The animals watched closely as Mr. Fox *drew the long stick out of the pot.*

"Yes," he announced proudly, "This soup is ready."

With one swoop of her big brown paw, Mother Bear cleared the snow from an old tree stump. It made a fine table. Mr. Fox filled the empty cans with hot soup. The animals had all the soup they could eat. And everyone agreed that it was, indeed, excellent soup.

"Now that we know how to make soup from snow," said Old Beaver, "we will never go hungry in the winter."

The other animals nodded their heads in agreement. Mr. Fox thanked his friends. The tricky old fox rubbed his bulging stomach and smiled as he walked off into the snowy forest.

Activity:

Provide an electric frying pan or cooking pot; a wooden stirring spoon; a ladle; strong plastic serrated knives; Styrofoam cups; and plastic spoons. Have children make snow soup, using the recipe on page 60.

Snow Soup for Kids

1. Have each child bring one vegetable to class.

2. Instruct the children to wash the vegetables and cut them into bite-sized pieces.

3. Place the cut vegetables into a large pan.

4. Add clean snow (or water). When the snow melts, there should be enough water to cover the vegetables.

5. Cook at medium heat.

6. Stir often and sing Mr. Fox's song.

7. Cook vegetables until they are slightly soft but still crisp.

8. Serve and eat. Delicious!

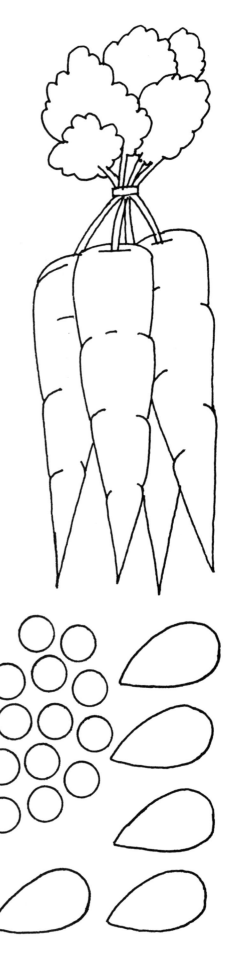

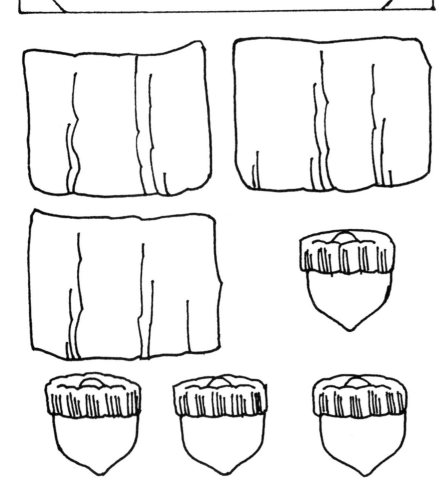

   Is Your Storytale Dragging? © 1988

A Special Yellow House

(adapted from an anonymous tale)

You will need a yellow pear with a stem, a paring knife, and a paper bag. Place the pear and knife in the paper bag, twist the top of the bag, and set it on a nearby table.

Stephen was visiting his grandmother. "There's nothing to do," he said.

Grandma looked at Stephen and said, "Once when I was a little girl, I said the same thing to my grandmother. She told me to go outside and look for a special house—a little yellow house with no doors or windows but with a chimney on top and a star inside. Maybe you can find that little house."

Stephen hurried outside and looked all around. He looked up and down both sides of the street. He ran to the corner and looked in both directions. But he couldn't find the special house.

Stephen called to the postman, "Have you seen a little yellow house with no doors or windows but with a chimney on top and a star inside?"

"I've seen many houses," said the postman, "but I've never seen a house like that."

"Thank you," said Stephen.

He saw the real estate woman putting up a "FOR SALE" sign on the vacant house. "Excuse me," Stephen said, "but have you seen a little yellow house with no doors or windows but with a chimney on top and a star inside?"

"I've seen many houses," she said, "but I've never seen one like that."

"Thank you," said Stephen as he strolled on down the street.

At the corner house, he saw two men carrying in a new refrigerator.

"Hello," said Stephen, "Have you ever seen a little yellow house with no doors or windows but with a chimney on top and a star inside?"

"We've seen many houses," said one of the men, "but we've never seen a house like that."

"Thanks," said Stephen as he started back up the street.

Stephen saw a woman reading the water meter across the street and called to her, "Have you seen a little yellow house with no doors or windows but with a chimney on top and a star inside?"

"I've seen many houses," the woman said, "but I've never seen one like that."

"Thanks," said Stephen. He turned and went inside. "Grandma, I've looked and looked, but I can't find the special yellow house."

"Well," said Grandma, "take these cookies and go sit under that big old tree in the backyard. If you think hard, I bet you'll find my special house."

Stephen sat down under the old tree and munched on his cookies. There was something on the ground near his foot. Stephen reached over and picked it up. *(Remove the pear from the bag and hold it up by the stem.)* He looked at the pear as he turned it around and around. Then he jumped up and ran into the house.

"Grandma, Grandma," he called, "I've found it. See, I've found the little yellow house with no doors or windows but with a chimney on top. Can I cut it open and see if there is a star inside?"

Grandma handed Stephen a knife. *(Remove knife from the bag.)* Carefully, Stephen cut around the midsection of the pear *(cut around the midsection, separating the stem and bottom end).* And inside, he found a . . . *(show the two halves)* star.

Activity:

Cut another pear lengthwise from the stem to the bottom end and look inside. If an apple is cut around the middle, you will also be able to see a star formation. Bring in several other fruits and have children predict which, if any, contain a star formation. Compare the seeds and seed beds of different fruits.

Part 6

Surprise Stories

Surprise Stories

Each story in this chapter contains an element of surprise. Yet, in each story you will find the surprise presented in a different way.

As you read the story "Dancing Paper," children will follow the motion of a paper streamer, a simple prop used to demonstrate different concepts of movement.

In "Gift from a Mermaid," the fascinating surprise prop is not revealed until the very end of the story.

In "Towel Doll," some animal friends of a young girl create, step-by-step, a special surprise doll for her.

"What a High-Flying Balloon!" introduces the story props in the first sentence, but the real surprise comes near the end of the story.

You will find a bit of magic weaving itself throughout the last three tales.

Three times during "The Muffin Man and His Wife," the swish of the storyteller's hand (and three Alka-Seltzer tablets) makes the water foam and bubble in preparation for the appearance of a wish-granting fish.

A few drops of food coloring dropped in water causes the bear in "Polar Bear, Polar Bear" to magically change colors before the eyes of your young audience.

In "The Unexpected, Disappearing Guest," a simple water drawing produces an unexpected guest. Near the end of the story, the process of evaporation causes the timely disappearance of the little visitor who saved the party. Could it have been a ghost?

Dancing Paper

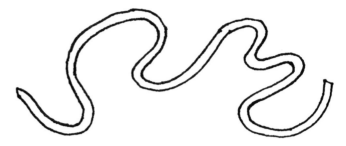

You will need a strip of three-inch crepe paper, four feet long. Hold one end of the paper strip and move it about as indicated in the story.

There was once a long strip of colored paper that wished to be a dancer. The paper did not know how to move. *(Stand stiffly, holding streamer motionless.)*

A breeze blew by and the paper started to move ever so gently. It began to move back and forth, faster and faster. Then it started swirling around and around. Up and down, faster and faster it went. The paper was dancing.

It dropped to the floor and nearly stopped moving. Then it wiggled back and forth on the floor. Around and around my feet it danced. In and out, between my legs, it danced. Then it twirled to my right, to my left, and over my head. Around and around my head it flew.

Then the paper began to spin. Slowly, slowly, it moved to the floor. But it rested for only a moment before it began twisting and turning, snapping and flipping.

It moved in small circles, and then in larger circles. It jumped up and then down. The paper danced between my feet, around my knees, and over my left shoulder. It flipped past my right ear and then spun about in front of my face.

Up, up, up it danced. The streamer danced higher and higher. I stood on my tiptoes, but the paper kept dancing toward the sky. It pulled and pulled and twisted and spun.

I could no longer hold on. The paper streamer danced off into the wind *(move the streamer behind you).*

I looked up and saw it moving gracefully among the clouds. And for all I know, it's still up there dancing, dancing, dancing.

Activity:

Give each child a paper streamer. Have the children do the actions as you retell the story. Children can also take turns giving directions for moving the streamers.

Gift from a Mermaid

You will need a large (one-gallon or larger), round, clear plastic bottle; blue food coloring; rubbing alcohol; mineral oil; paraffin wax; and a large paper bag. Fill half the bottle with mineral oil. Add blue food coloring until the oil is deep blue. Slowly pour in rubbing alcohol until the bottle is full. Screw the lid on tightly. For added protection, seal the cap with paraffin wax. Place the bottle in the bag.

In a small village in a faraway land, there lived an old woman. "Ah–nalee, Ah–nalee, come here," she called.

The little girl came running and knelt down by the side of the old woman's bed.

The old woman lifted the lid from a small jeweled box and took out a gold coin. "Tomorrow will be your tenth birthday," she said. "Take this gold coin and go down to the sea. When the sun is high overhead, toss the coin into the water."

At noon the next day, Ah-nalee went down to the sea. She threw the coin into the water and waited. The cool, blue water lapped at her bare toes. In and out, in and out, went the waves.

Then up through the waves came a beautiful mermaid. She spoke to the little girl. "Long ago your great-grandmother befriended me and I gave her a gold wishing coin. I told her that if her first great-grand-daughter, on her tenth birthday, would return it to the sea, I would grant the girl a birthday wish. What is your wish?"

Ah-nalee quickly answered, "Give me all the gold coins in the world."

"I cannot do that," said the mermaid, "for then no one else would have any. They would not be able to buy food or clothes or have a place to live." The mermaid went back into the water.

The cool, blue waves swished higher and higher. They lapped at the little girl's feet. In and out, in and out, they went. Up through the water came the mermaid. "Do you have another wish?" she asked.

Ah-nalee answered, "Give me all the flowers in the world."

"I cannot do that," said the mermaid, "for then no one else would be able to smell their sweetness or see their beauty." The mermaid went back into the water.

The cool, blue waves swished higher and higher. They lapped at the little girl's ankles. In and out, in and out, they went. Up through the water came the mermaid. "Do you have another wish?" she asked.

Ah-nalee answered, "Give me all the waves in the sea."

"I cannot do that," said the mermaid. "The waves are part of the sea. They stretch out across the world and they belong to all the people." The mermaid went back into the sea.

The cool, blue waves swished higher and higher. They lapped around the little girl's legs. In and out, in and out, they went. Up through the water came the mermaid. "Do you have another wish?" she asked.

"Yes," Ah–nalee answered. "My wish is that everyone have a few gold coins to spend, pretty flowers to smell, and ocean waves to roll in around their feet."

The mermaid smiled and went back into the sea.

The cool, blue waves swished higher and higher. They lapped at the little girl's knees. In and out, in and out, they went. Then a great gust of wind came and blew the waves far out to sea.

Ah–nalee knew that she would never see the mermaid again. As she turned and started home, something rolled against her feet. The little girl looked down and there in the sand was her birthday gift. The mermaid had left Ah–nalee her very own . . . *(remove the bottle from the bag, hold it flat, and slowly tip the bottle back and forth to give the effect of ocean waves)* blue wave.

Activity:

Have the children bring in a jar or bottle. Provide mineral oil, blue food coloring, and rubbing alcohol so they can make their own "bottle waves."

Towel Doll

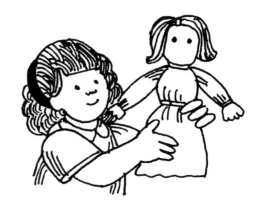

You will need a lightweight, medium-size blue towel; a red scarf; three 10" pieces of brown ribbon; ten 12" pieces of yellow yarn; and two acorns. Place the lengths of yarn side by side and tie them together at the center to form the hairpiece. Keep the props concealed in a box or bag until you are ready to use them. See illustrations on page 69 to form the doll.

Little Pandora walked slowly down to the stream. Each day she came to the same spot. She would sit on the grass and sing for hours.

It was here, too, that Beaver, Rabbit, Squirrel, and Crow came to drink fresh water. They listened to the sweet sounds of her voice.

"I think Pandora is lonely," said Rabbit, "for her songs are always sad."

"And she never smiles," said Squirrel.

"I wish we could do something for her," said Beaver.

Crow said, "Tomorrow at sunrise, let us have a meeting under the old tree that grows deep in the forest." The animals nodded.

The next morning, they met as planned. "We must do something," said Squirrel.

"But how can we help?" asked Rabbit.

Just then a gust of wind blew an old blue towel down the path, right in front of the animals. *(Place towel on the table.)* They looked at the towel and then whispered among themselves. Quickly the four friends set to work.

Crow picked up the towel and folded it like this. *(Fold towel in half, lengthwise.)* Rabbit hurried off to

her rabbit hole and brought back the red scarf that she had found last week stuck in the berry bush. She tied it like this. *(Tie scarf to form neck. Let scarf dangle to form arms.)*

Beaver stripped three strong strings from the inside of a piece of bark. He tied the towel like this. *(Tie ribbon to form the waist.)* He tied one short strip here, and the other here. *(Tie ribbon to form the hands.)*

Squirrel scampered off and brought two shiny acorns and pushed them into the towel, right here. *(Push acorns into towel folds to form eyes.)* Crow flew off. He returned with a beak full of golden corn silk and placed it right here. *(Place the yarn hair on the head.)*

They carried the towel doll down to the stream and placed it where the little girl always sat.

Pandora walked down to her favorite spot. She glanced down and saw the doll. She smiled as she picked it up and hugged it in her arms. *(Pick up doll and hug it.)* She looked around and saw all the animals watching her. Then she began to sing. Pandora sang more sweetly than she had ever sung before, and for the first time, her songs were happy ones.

For many years after that, she came to the stream to sing for her animal friends, and she always smiled and carried the towel doll.

Activity:

Provide pieces of old bed sheets, ribbons, and yarn for the children to use in making their own boy or girl doll. Felt scraps can be glued on for the facial features.

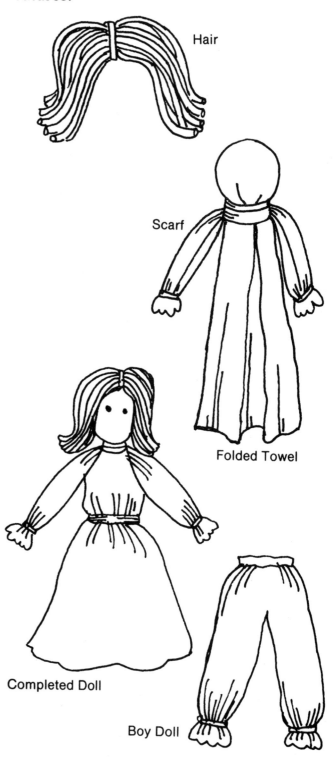

Hair

Scarf

Folded Towel

Completed Doll

Boy Doll

Separate the skirt and tie off with ribbon to make pant legs.

What a High-Flying Balloon!

You will need one air-filled balloon in each of the following colors: blue, pink, white, and orange; and one helium-filled red balloon. Tie a 24" piece of string to each balloon. Attach the strings to the back of a chair and take it outdoors for the storytelling.

Once there were a bunch of balloons tied to a fence. They were talking among themselves about who would fly the highest.

"If I were free," said the blue balloon, "I would fly the highest." So it pulled and twisted and jerked until it was free. *(Release the blue balloon.)* The blue balloon bounced a bit but never got off the ground.

"If I were free," said the pink balloon, "I would fly the highest." So it pulled and twisted and jerked until it was free. *(Release the pink balloon.)* The pink balloon bounced a bit but never got off the ground.

"If I were free," said the white balloon, "I would fly the highest." So it pulled and twisted and jerked until it was free. *(Release the white balloon.)* The white balloon bounced a bit but never got off the ground.

"If I were free," said the orange balloon, "I would fly the highest." So it pulled and twisted and jerked until it was free. *(Release the orange balloon.)* The orange balloon bounced a bit but never got off the ground.

The red balloon didn't say anything. It just pulled and twisted and jerked until it was free. *(Release the red balloon.)* The red balloon took right off into the sky. Up, up, up it went.

The other balloons watched. Higher and higher the red balloon floated. Across the fence, over the trees, and above the rooftops it flew.

The red balloon dipped and bowed and smiled down at its friends. It knew all the time that it would fly the highest because it was filled with a special substance, a gas called helium that is lighter than air.

The other balloons watched the red balloon float across the rivers and over the mountain tops. It went higher and higher. It traveled for many miles until it was finally out of sight. The blue balloon, the pink balloon, the white balloon, and the orange balloon never saw the red balloon again.

Activity:

Have children write notes and attach them to helium-filled balloons. Plan a special time to release the balloons.

The Muffin Man and His Wife

(an adaptation of a folktale)

You will need a large, clear glass bowl half-full of water; blue food coloring; and nine Alka-Seltzer tablets. Add blue food coloring to the water, and keep the props out of sight until needed.

Once there was a muffin man who lived with his wife in a small village. Every morning they got up very early. The wife spent many hours in her tiny kitchen mixing and stirring and then baking the muffins. The muffin man loaded the fresh muffins into his cart and pushed it up and down the street.

"Muffins for sale. Muffins for sale," he called out.

It was hard work for the man and woman and they made only a little money. One day the woman was sick and couldn't bake any muffins, so the old man decided to go fishing. *(Set the bowl of water on a table near you.)* Right away he caught a nice fish.

"If you'll throw me back in the water," said the fish, "I will grant you a wish."

The man threw the fish back into the water. "Come tomorrow at the same time," said the fish. "Stir the water with your hand and I'll appear and grant your wish."

The muffin man went home and told his wife what had happened.

"Ask the fish for a little muffin shop of our own," she said.

The next day the muffin man went back to the pond. He put his hand in the water and stirred it around and around. *(Conceal three Alka-Seltzer tablets in your hand. Place your hand in the water and stir gently.)* The water bubbled and foamed, and the fish appeared.

"We would like a little muffin shop of our own," said the muffin man.

"Go home and go to bed," said the fish.

The man and woman went to bed. The next morning they found themselves in a beautiful muffin shop. There was a new oven in the kitchen, and a baker so the muffin man's wife did not have to work. There were tables where people could sit to eat the fresh muffins. The man no longer had to peddle muffins on the street.

But the muffin man's wife said, "Go back and tell the fish that we want a larger shop with five ovens and ten bakers. We want rows and rows of tables."

The next day, the muffin man went back to the pond. He put his hand in the water and stirred it around and around. *(Conceal three Alka-Seltzer tablets in your hand. Place your hand in the water and stir gently.)* The water bubbled and foamed, and the fish appeared.

The man said, "We want a larger shop with five ovens and ten bakers and rows and rows of tables."

"Go home and go to bed," said the fish.

The man and the woman went to bed. The next morning, they found themselves in a much larger shop. There were five ovens and ten bakers. There were many rooms, with enough tables and chairs for a hundred people to sit and eat muffins.

But the muffin man's wife said, "Go back and tell the fish that we want a shop as big as a castle, with

fifty bakers. We want tables in every room so that a thousand people can sit and eat our muffins."

The man went back to the pond. He put his hand in the water and stirred it around and around. *(Conceal three Alka-Seltzer tablets in your hand. Place your hand in the water and stir gently.)* The water bubbled and foamed, and the fish appeared.

"We want a shop as big as a castle, with fifty bakers," said the man. "And we want tables for a thousand people."

"Go home and go to bed," said the fish.

The muffin man and his wife went to bed. The next morning, they awoke to find themselves back in their tiny kitchen with the old oven. And the muffin man never saw the fish again.

Activity:

Using a box of muffin mix, have the class make muffins.

Polar Bear, Polar Bear

You will need a plastic bear-shaped honey bottle (or a bear-shaped baby bottle, or a plastic cup with a bear's face pasted to the front); yellow, blue, and red food coloring; an eyedropper; a sheet of white construction paper; and a one-ounce bottle of chlorine bleach. (Keep the lid of the bleach container tightly closed and out of reach of the children.) Fill the bear-shaped bottle to within one-half inch of the top with water. Before you start the story, instruct the children to clap their hands and stamp their feet after each of the polar bear's tricks.

Once there was a beautiful white polar bear who lived in the zoo. *(Set bear filled with water on the table and place the white sheet of paper behind it so the bear appears white.)* Every day, the children came to the zoo to watch the bear. He would sit up, balancing himself with his feet in the air. Then he would roll in the grass, sit up, and clap his big furry paws. He enjoyed performing for the children. When he finished, the children would *clap their hands and stamp their feet.*

One day Polar Bear stood by his fence watching the workmen paint the nearby buildings. Three cans of paint were left by the fence when the workmen went home. Polar Bear reached through the fence and grabbed the cans. That night, he dipped his big paw into the first can of paint and painted himself— *(Squeeze three drops of yellow food coloring into the water and let the children supply the color word.)*

The next day, the children came and Polar Bear did his tricks. The children *clapped their hands and stamped their feet* and said:

> Polar Bear, Polar Bear, your color's too bright.
> We liked you best when your color was white.

That night, the bear dipped his big paw into the second can of paint and painted himself— *(Squeeze three drops of blue food coloring into the water and let the children supply the color word.)*

The next day, the children came and Polar Bear did his tricks. The children *clapped their hands and stamped their feet* and said:

> Polar Bear, Polar Bear, your color's too bright.
> We liked you best when your color was white.

That night, the bear dipped his big paw into the third can of paint and painted himself—(*Squeeze three drops of red food coloring into the water and let the children supply the color word.*)

The next day, the children came and Polar Bear did his tricks. The children *clapped their hands and stamped their feet* and said:

> Polar Bear, Polar Bear, your color's too bright.
> We liked you best when your color was white.

The bear looked at the children. The children looked at the bear. Polar Bear jumped into the water (*continue with the story as you add the chlorine bleach, drop by drop, until the water is clear*) and swam and swam. He went down so deep that the children couldn't see him. Up and down in the water he swam. Finally he climbed out.

The children *clapped their hands and stamped their feet* and said:

> Polar Bear, Polar Bear, your color's just right.
> We love you, Polar Bear, so pretty and white.

The bear decided never again to change his color. After all, polar bears are supposed to be white— aren't they?

(*Empty and rinse the containers immediately. Chlorine can burn.*)

Activity:

Provide water; food coloring in squeeze bottles (red, yellow, blue, green); plastic measuring cups; and a Styrofoam egg carton for each child. Have the children use a measuring cup to fill each egg cup half-full of water. Let them experiment by squeezing drops of food coloring into the water. Instruct them to add one drop at a time and to see how many different colors they can make. Older children can record the number of drops added and the results, along with their observations.

Plastic Cup Bear

Bear head glued to the top of the cup.

The Unexpected, Disappearing Guest

You will need a glass of water, a long cotton swab, and a large sheet of black construction paper on an easel. Dip the swab in the water until it is saturated. Draw the ghost on page 76 as indicated in the story. Do a practice test in advance to help you time the drawing so the ghost will have disappeared when the story ends.

Fernando was having his first party—a Halloween party. Mother let him invite five friends and helped him plan the games and refreshments. Fernando was busy all week getting ready. Now it was time for the party.

"I'll be upstairs with the baby. Call if you need me," said Mother.

Knock. Knock. Fernando opened the door. There stood Maria in her witch costume. "Come in," he said. "You are the first one to arrive."

Knock. Knock. Fernando opened the door. There stood Eugene in his cowboy costume. "Come in," said Fernando. "You are the second one to arrive."

Knock. Knock. Fernando opened the door. There stood Bruce in his hobo costume. "Come in," said Fernando. "You are the third one to arrive."

Knock. Knock. Fernando opened the door. There stood Lee Ann in her Minnie Mouse costume. "Come in," he said. "You are the fourth one to arrive."

Knock. Knock. Fernando opened the door. There stood Barbara in her Cinderella costume. "Come in," he said. "You are the fifth one to arrive."

"Everyone is here," called Fernando. "We are ready to play the games." Suddenly the children heard a soft knock, knock. "Who could it be? I only invited five people," said Fernando.

Maria looked out the window. "Look," she said. "It's a tiny ghost." Fernando opened the door. *(Start drawing the ghost as you continue the story.)* The tiny ghost was crying.

"What's the matter?" asked Eugene.

The tiny ghost wiped its eyes and looked up at the children. "Our family has been out ghosting all night and I'm tired of flying around. I saw your light and . . . and . . ."

"Come in, come in," the children said. *(Complete the ghost drawing.)*

The tiny ghost joined the children in bobbing for apples and in playing Witch, Witch and the Hot Chili Pepper game.

"It's time for the special event," said Fernando. "It's time to play the Piñata game."

Fernando hung the giant orange pumpkin piñata on the ceiling hook. Everyone took turns swinging with the broomstick. They tried and tried, but none of them could break the smiling piñata. The tired, unhappy children sat down on the floor.

Suddenly there was a sound like the blowing of the wind. Then, pop! Pop! Pop! The giant orange pumpkin piñata had split apart. The children laughed and screamed as the candy and toys fell into their laps. They looked up at the battered piñata and saw the tiny ghost smile as he released his arms from around the orange pumpkin.

But before they could thank him, he had disappeared.

Activity:

Provide children with 8½″ × 11″ sheets of black construction paper, small cotton swabs, and water. Let them experiment with water drawings. Encourage the children to write a story to accompany the drawing. Younger children can make a recording of their stories.

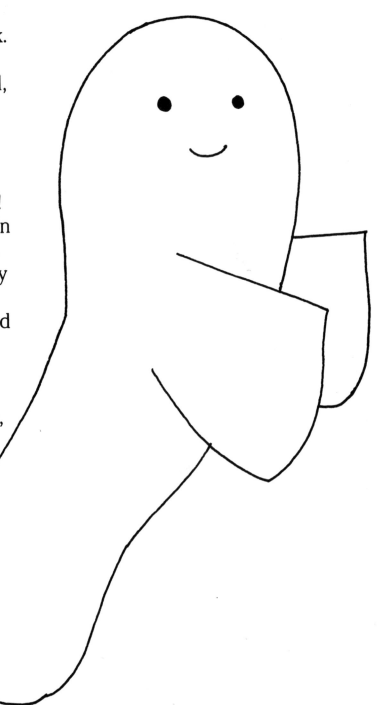